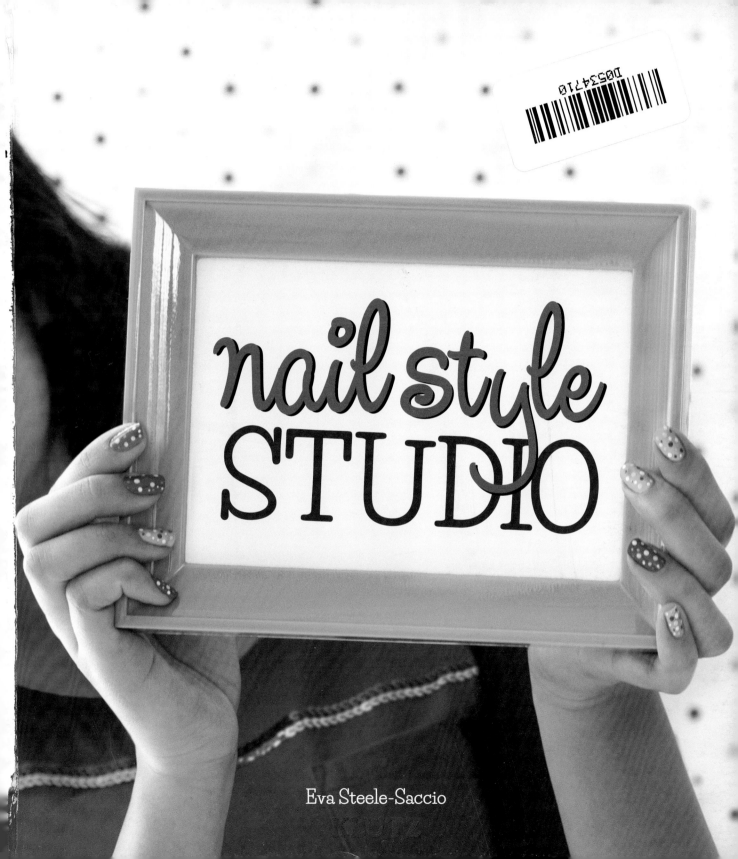

nail style STUDIO

Eva Steele-Saccio

KLUTZ

Contents

DOTS

17
POLKA-DOT
SWAP

18
CUTE
CONFETTI

19
LACY DOTS

20
DOT BUILDUP

22
A LOTTA
DOTS

24
DOTTED
CHEVRON

24
FANCY
FLORETS

26
HALF-MOONS

CUTE STUFF

29
PLAYFUL
PANDA

30
SNOWY
PENGUIN

32
TASTY
CUPCAKE

34
SNEAKY
SNEAKER

34
BUTTERFLY
WING

36
ADORABLE
OWL

38
FRIENDLY
FLAMINGO

PICTURE NAILS

41
CITY
SKYLINE

42
SHARK
ATTACK!

44
LOVEBIRDS
ON A WIRE

46
TROPICAL
BEACH

STICK-ON STENCILS

50
SLEEK
STRIPE

52
DOTTED X

52
LIGHTNING
BOLT

54
ZANY
ZIGZAG

56
FRENCH
TIPS

57
STAR &
HEART

58
GRAPHIC
CHEVRON

what you get

DOTTING TOOL

PRACTICE POLISH

.17 oz / 5 ml

.17 oz / 5 ml

.17 oz / 5 ml

.17 oz / 5 ml

.17 oz / 5 ml

PRACTICE
Polish

PRACTICE
Polish

PRACTICE
Polish

PRACTICE
Polish

PRACTICE
Polish

PRACTICE
Polish

STICK-ON STENCILS

If you spill the practice polish, quickly clean up with warm soapy water to minimize staining. Don't paint over open wounds. If you develop a rash, stop using the polish and talk to your doctor. And (obviously) don't eat the polish or give it to someone who might.

Practice...

Practice polish is exactly what it sounds like: nail polish for practicing the designs in this book. It's made to come off easily. Once the polish is dry, you can just peel it off or wash it off with soap and water. Use it when you're doing a design for the first time. Keep painting with the practice polish until you are happy with the way your art looks.

...Makes Perfect!

After you've perfected the design, you may want to switch to regular nail polish (make sure you get an OK from an adult first). Regular polish — the type you buy at the drugstore — will last a lot longer than practice polish. You can do most of the designs in this book with any colors you like. If you don't already have black and white, it would be good to add them to your collection. A clear base coat and top coat are useful, and you will also need nail polish remover.

the basics

The next few pages walk you through how to prep and paint your nails. Read carefully — learning the basics now will make it much easier later.

Give yourself a manicure

This simple manicure will give you a nice clean canvas for your nail designs. If you'd rather jump right into painting, it's totally fine to skip this part.

WHAT YOU NEED

- cotton balls or pads
- nail polish remover
- nail brush
- nail clippers
- nail file
- nail buffer
- small bowl of warm water
- olive oil
- lotion

CLEAN

Remove old polish from your nails. If you've used practice polish, peel off the paint or wash your nails with warm, soapy water. Clean under your nails, too. A nail brush will help.

TRIM

Trim your nails so they are all about the same length. It will be a little easier to do the designs if your nails are long, but don't worry if they're on the shorter side.

FILE

Place the nail file just under the tip of your nail. Hold it at a 45-degree angle and make long, even strokes. Always file in one direction — don't saw back and forth.

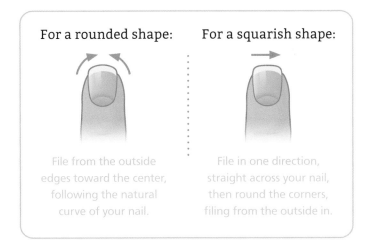

For a rounded shape:

File from the outside edges toward the center, following the natural curve of your nail.

For a squarish shape:

File in one direction, straight across your nail, then round the corners, filing from the outside in.

BUFF

There are many types of nail buffers, from blocks to boards. All buffers have at least two surfaces, a rough side (for smoothing) and a softer side (for shining). Use the rough side to make light strokes over your nail, going in one direction. Then make light strokes with the soft side to bring out the shine.

SOAK

If you want to push back your cuticles, soak your fingertips in a bowl of warm water. Then massage a little olive oil into your cuticles, using your thumb to gently push them back. Wash your hands to remove the oil.

MOISTURIZE

Rub some lotion into your hands. Wait for the lotion to soak in (about ten minutes). Beautiful!

ALL SHAPES AND SIZES

Everyone's nails are unique, so don't worry if your nails look different than those in this book. The designs should work on all nail types, but you may need to play around to find the proportions that work best for you.

Getting started

Here's some important info about how to follow the instructions in this book and set up your workspace.

ABOUT THE ART

You'll notice that the step-by-step illustrations in this book are "upside-down." That's because the finished nail art is meant to face the person admiring your manicure.

Tip

Base

The illustrations show what the art looks like from your view as you paint your nails — looking down at your hand laid flat on the table. It might be a little awkward to follow at first, but soon you'll get the hang of it.

The art is upside-down to you, but it will be right side-up to someone looking at your nails.

A HELPING HAND

Unless you're an ambidextrous superhuman, you'll probably need help painting your dominant hand. Team up with a friend or adult — it's more fun anyway. To see the illustrations from the correct perspective, the person doing your nails should look at the book upside down. You can read the directions to her aloud.

SET UP YOUR STUDIO

Cover a flat surface (a table or a counter) with newspaper or an old dish towel. Then arrange your polish so you can reach it easily but won't knock it over. Place a couple of cotton pads and a bowl of water (or a bottle of nail polish remover if using regular nail polish) nearby. You'll use these to clean your tool. You also need a palette for the polish. A piece of paper folded in half works well.

How to paint your nails

Most of the designs in this book start with a solid coat of polish.
The key is using the right amount of polish — just enough
to cover your nail without getting gloppy.

1 Dip the brush into the bottle. Wipe it against the inside of the bottle neck to remove extra polish. Your brush should be thinly coated — not dripping.

When using regular polish, apply a clear base coat (and wait for it to dry) before adding the solid coat.

2 Paint a strip down the center of your nail, starting at the base and brushing toward the tip.

3 Now paint one side of your nail...

...and then the other side. Let the polish dry.

tip Always cap your bottles immediately after you're done using them.

4 Add a second solid coat unless the directions say not to. Wait for that to dry, too. Now you're ready to add the details of your design.

To make a manicure with regular polish last longer, add a clear top coat after your design has dried.

DRY TIME

It's really important to let the polish dry between steps. Because every polish is different, there's no hard rule for how long you should wait. To speed up drying, you can use a blow dryer on the cool setting.

Using the dotter

This is your dotter. You'll be using it to make dots, lines, and shapes. The tool has two ends: a round **ball** and a sharp **point**.

The **ball** makes big dots and larger shapes.

Before you begin the designs in the book, practice using your tool. Read the next couple of pages, then make lines, shapes, and dots on your nails. Keep practicing until you're happy with the results.

The **point** makes small dots, fine lines, and other details.

Instead of dipping the tool directly into the polish bottle, you're going to work from a paper palette.

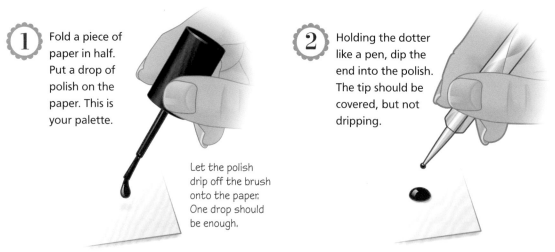

1 Fold a piece of paper in half. Put a drop of polish on the paper. This is your palette.

Let the polish drip off the brush onto the paper. One drop should be enough.

2 Holding the dotter like a pen, dip the end into the polish. The tip should be covered, but not dripping.

MAKING LINES

Lightly dab the polish across your nail to make a line.

Don't worry if your line looks bumpy at first. Keep practicing, and soon you'll get a more even look.

LINE THICKNESS

To get a fine line, use the point of the dotter. To get a thick line, use the ball.

MAKING SHAPES

1 First, dab the outline of the shape.

2 Then, fill in the inside of the shape, also by dabbing.

tip
You can fill in larger shapes with the polish brush, too.

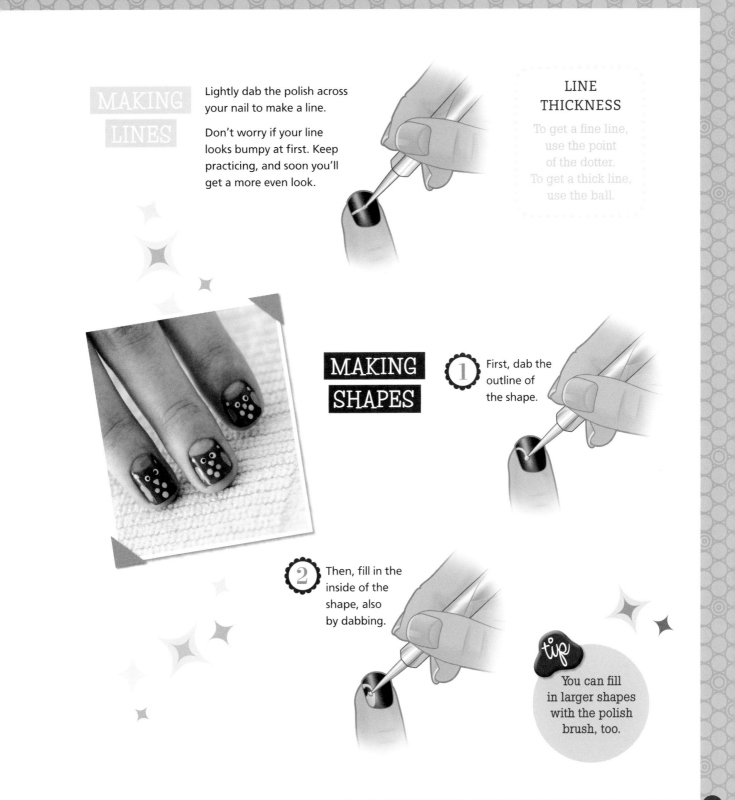

MAKING DOTS

1 Add a fresh drop of polish to your palette. Dip the the dotter into the polish, so the tip is covered but not dripping.

If the polish dries up or gets sticky, add another drop.

2 Press the dotter onto your nail. Then lift it up. You've made a dot.

tip To get nice, round dots, you'll need to re-dip the tool in the polish as you go. How often will depend on your dotting style, so experiment and find what works best for you.

DOT SIZE

If the directions tell you to make a **big** dot, use the **ball** of the dotter. If they say to make a **small** dot, use the **point** of the dotter. The exact size of each dot will change depending on how much paint you use and how much pressure you apply. Light pressure and less paint make a delicate dot. More pressure and more paint make a bolder dot.

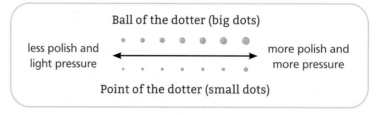

Ball of the dotter (big dots)

less polish and light pressure ← → more polish and more pressure

Point of the dotter (small dots)

{*Cleaning the dotter*}

It's important to clean the tool when you switch colors or are finished using it. Here's how...

◆ Moisten a cotton pad with water (if you're using practice polish) or nail polish remover (if you're using regular polish). Wipe off the end of the tool on the damp cotton, making sure it's totally clean.

◆ Check your cotton pad periodically to make sure it's still wet. If you clean the tool with a dry pad, strands of cotton will stick to the dotter and then get caught in the polish or on your nail. Not good!

tip
Keep the cotton pad nearby while you work. You'll be cleaning your tool often.

{Design Styles}

There are several ways you can combine the designs in this book to get the look you want. Here are a few...

Simple

For this timeless style, paint every nail with the identical design and colors.

elegant

Accent

Paint all your nails the same, except the "accent" nail (usually the ring or index finger), which has a different design or color.

unique

Mix &
MATCH

Make your manicure stand out by painting each nail with a different design. Using the same color palette (three to four colors that alternate from nail to nail), brings the look together.

playful

Dots {

All the designs in this section use the dotter to achieve simple but stunning styles. Ready, set... dot!

POLKA-DOT Swap

1

pinky · thumb

Paint your nails in alternating colors. Then add a second coat. Wait for the polish to dry.

2

tip Start dotting at the base of your nail and work your way up.

Make **big** dots on each nail, using the color you didn't use for the solid coat.

Try using three colors on two hands. The shared color (black in this photo) brings the designs together nicely.

CUTE Confetti

WHAT YOU NEED
- Polish for the solid coat
- 3 colors of polish for the dots
- Dotter

1

Paint your nails with two coats of the solid color. Wait for the polish to dry.

2

Use the first dot color to make two **big** dots and three **small** dots on each nail, anywhere you like.

3

Repeat with the other two dot colors: Make two **big** dots and three **small** dots on each nail.

tip

Shorter nails may need fewer dots, and longer nails may need more.

LACY Dots

WHAT YOU NEED

- Polish for the solid coat
- 2 colors of polish for the dots
- Dotter

1

Paint your nails with two coats of the solid color. Wait for the polish to dry.

tip This design looks best with dainty dots. Use a little less polish than usual and press gently when dotting.

2

Start dotting at the tip of your nail and work your way down.

Make a line of **big** dots in the first dot color, leaving space between them.

3

Shorter nails may need fewer dots.

Using the second dot color, add **small** dots between the big dots.

{ For a different look, try doing this design across your nails.

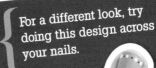

DOT Buildup

The dots in this design build from one finger to the next, starting with one column on your pinky and ending with five on your thumb.

WHAT YOU NEED
- Polish for the solid coat
- 3 colors of polish for the dots
- Dotter

①

Paint your nails with two coats of the solid color. Wait for the polish to dry.

② pinky

Using the first dot color, make a line of **big** dots on the left side of each nail.

tip Remember to clean the tool before switching colors. If cotton sticks to the metal, use more water or polish remover. Pick the cotton off the tool and clean it again.

③ ring finger

The lines should be close together, but not touching.

Use the second dot color to make another line of **big** dots on your ring finger, middle finger, index finger, and thumb (skip your pinky).

4

middle finger

Use the third dot color to make a line of **big** dots on your middle finger, index finger, and thumb.

tip When the polish gets sticky or dries out, add a new drop to your palette. Re-dip the tool frequently to get nice, round dots.

5

index finger

Make these two columns the same color.

Now go back to the second dot color. Make a line of **big** dots on your index finger and thumb.

6

thumb

Make these two columns the same color.

Using the first dot color, make one last line of **big** dots on your thumb.

A LOTTA Dots

For this design, you'll use three colors of dots in two sizes. The dotting takes a while, but all the *oohs* and *ahhs* your nails will get are well worth it.

tip Remember to add more polish to your palette as it dries out. Re-dip the tool often to get nice, round dots.

1

Paint your nails with two coats of the solid color. Wait for the polish to dry.

2

Use the first dot color to make a line of **big** dots on each nail, anywhere you like.

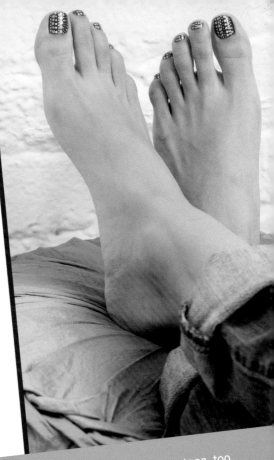

3

Make your dots in the same order or switch it up from nail to nail.

Use the same color to make a line of **small** dots on each nail, also anywhere you like.

4

tip

Remember to clean the tool before switching colors, using plenty of water or polish remover.

Do the same thing with the second dot color: On each nail, make a line of **big** dots, then a line of **small** dots.

{ This design looks cute on toes, too. Since your toenails are smaller, try using two colors instead of three.

5

The lines should be close together, but not touching.

Repeat again with the third dot color. Don't worry if you can't fit exactly six lines on each nail — the design will still be stunning.

6

Fill in this space.

If necessary, fill in any empty space with a line of small dots in any color you like.

DOTTED
Chevron

WHAT YOU NEED

- Polish for the solid coat
- 2 colors of polish for the dots
- Dotter

1

Paint your nails with two coats of the solid color. Wait for the polish to dry.

FANCY
Florets

WHAT YOU NEED

- Polish for the solid coat
- 2 colors of polish for the dots
- Dotter

1

Paint your nails with two coats of the solid color. Wait for the polish to dry.

2

Leave space between the dot and the edge of your nail.

Use the first dot color to make three **big** dots on your nail: at the top left, middle, and bottom right.

3

The small dots go at the top, bottom, left, and right of the big dot.

Use the second dot color to make four **small** dots around each big dot. These are the petals.

tip This design works best with delicate dots. When dotting, use a little less polish than usual. The less pressure you apply, the daintier your dot will be.

{ Try alternating the direction of the chevrons from nail to nail. }

2

Use the first dot color to make a **big** dot in the middle of your nail, just above the base.

3

Make two **big** dots that angle up and to the left of the first one.

4

Make sure the dots on the right line up with those on the left.

Make two more **big** dots that angle up and to the right of the first one. You've made the first chevron.

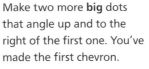

5

Make a **small** dot in the second color, right above the big middle dot. Then add three more **small** dots on each side.

FLORET BOUQUET

Turn your florets into a beautiful bouquet with these simple steps.

1

Make six or so **big** dots on your nail. Leave room for the petals.

2

Remember to press lightly when you dot.

Now add **small** dots for the petals.

HALF-Moons

1

Paint your nails with two coats of the solid color. Wait for the polish to dry.

2

pinky   thumb

Your dots don't have to match the picture exactly.

Make five **big** dots in a loose arc on the left side of your pinky, middle finger, and thumb. Then make five **big** dots in a loose arc on the right side of your ring and index fingers.

3

Start making a curved shape on each finger by adding **small** dots in the **second** dot color.

Don't worry about creating a perfect curve. Variation looks pretty.

4

Shorter nails may need fewer dots.

Now fill in the curved shape with **small** dots in the **first** dot color.

Cute stuff

{ Irresistible owls, fluffy cupcakes, and fashionable flamingos — these designs are seriously adorable.

PLAYFUL Panda

WHAT YOU NEED

- Polish for the solid coat
- White polish
- Black polish
- Dotter

1

Paint your nails with two coats of the solid color. Wait for the polish to dry completely.

2

You may need two coats of white.

When the solid coat is dry, use the ball of the dotter to outline a white half-circle. Fill it in using the dotter or polish brush.

3

Use the ball of the dotter to make two black circles for ears. Then make two smaller black circles just above the ears. These are the eye rings.

4

Use the ball of the dotter to make a black dot for the nose near the tip of your nail. Wait for all the black polish to dry.

5

Using the ball of the dotter, make two white dots in the middle of the black eye rings. Let the polish dry.

6

Now, use the point of the dotter to make two **small** black dots on top of the white dots. Your panda has peepers!

SNOWY Penguin

1

Paint your nails with two coats of the solid color. Wait for the polish to dry completely.

2

When the solid coat is dry, use the ball of the dotter to outline a tall, black oval. Fill it in using the dotter or polish brush. Let the polish dry completely.

3

Leave space here for the eyes.

Use the ball of the dotter to make a smaller white oval on top of the black oval. You may need two coats of white.

4

Make two **big** white dots on the black oval. Let the polish dry.

5

Make two **small** black dots on top of the white dots. The eyes are done.

6

Use the point of the dotter to make a small triangle in the beak color. Squawk!

Let your penguin fly solo — paint your non-accent nails with just snow.

7

To make a half-dot, place the ball of the dotter part way off your nail, then press down.

Use the ball of the dotter to make two half-dots in the beak color on the tip of your nail. These are the feet.

8

Now let it snow... Make **small** dots around the penguin in the snow color.

PARTY PENGUINS

Dress up your penguins with bows or bow ties. Use the point of the dotter to make two tiny triangles facing each other.

TASTY
Cupcake

1

Paint from just above the middle of your nail toward the tip.

Paint the top of your nail in the wrapper color. Let it dry, then add another coat. Wait for the second coat to dry, too.

2

You may need two coats of white.

Use the ball of the dotter to make a white half-circle below the wrapper, leaving some space above the base of your nail. This is the frosting.

Place the dots half on the pink and half on the white.

Make a line of **big** white dots along the straight edge of the half-circle. Wait for all the white to dry.

{ Switch up your frosting and wrapper colors to make your own little bakery...

Use the point of the dotter to make four white stripes on the wrapper.

...or use the cupcake as an accent nail. }

Make four **small** dots in the first sprinkle color, then add four more in the second sprinkle color.

Top your cupcake off with a heart. Make two **big** pink dots near each other. Then use the point of the dotter to connect them.

SNEAKY Sneaker

{ **WHAT YOU NEED**
- Polish for the sneaker
- White polish
- Black polish
- Dotter }

1

Paint your nails with two coats of the sneaker color. Wait for the polish to dry completely.

{ **WHAT YOU NEED**
- Black polish
- Polish for wing accents (bright colors work best)
- White polish
- Dotter }

Butterfly WING

1

Paint your nails with two coats of black. Wait for the polish to dry completely.

2

Make sure the solid coat is dry. On the right edge of your nail, make a long, skinny shape in the wing accent color.

tip Don't worry about making your shapes look exactly like the picture. Variation looks pretty and natural — just like a real butterfly.

You may need two coats of white.

Use the ball of the dotter or polish brush to make a white oval on the tip of your nail. This is the shoe's toe.

Make sure the right dots line up with the left dots.

Make three **big** white dots on the left side of your nail and three on the right.

For shoelaces, use the point of the dotter to make a white X between the top four dots. Make another X below it. Let the polish dry.

Let the white toe dry completely before adding the line.

Make **small** black dots on top of the white dots. Then use the point of the dotter to draw a curved black line along the toe.

{ WING IT
Try flipping the design to make a pair of wings that face each other. }

3

Paint the middle shape first.

Use the ball of the dotter to make three more shapes next to the first shape. Leave some space on the left side of your nail.

4

Make **small** white dots on the left side of your nail. Use light pressure.

ADORABLE
Owl

WHAT YOU NEED

- Polish for the owl body
- Polish for the wings, feathers, and ears
- Polish for the beak
- White polish
- Black polish
- Dotter

1

Use the point of the dotter to draw an arc near the base of your nail in the owl body color.

2

Use the dotter to fill in the corners.

Using the same color, paint your nail above the arc. Let the polish dry, then add another coat. Wait for the second coat to dry, too.

USE A STICK-ON STENCIL

If you're working with regular polish, try using a stick-on stencil as a guide. Place a half-circle sticker at the base of your nail. Paint your nail, covering the edge of the sticker. Wait for the polish to dry. Add another coat, then remove the sticker immediately. (See page 49 for more stick-on stencil tips).

Press the edge of the sticker against your nail firmly.

3

Use the ball of the dotter to make a half-circle on each side of your nail in the wing color.

4

The ears go in the corners of the head.

Using the same color, make three **big** dots near the tip of your nail for feathers. Then use the point of the dotter to make two tiny triangles for ears.

tip

Having trouble making the owl's ears? Try small dots instead of triangles.

5

Make two **big** white dots for eyes. Let the polish dry.

6

Now make two **small** black dots for pupils.

7

Use the point of the dotter to make a triangle in the beak color. Hoot hoot!

{ **IT'S ALL ABOUT THE**
PEEPERS!
Give your owl personality by playing with the placement of the pupils.

FRIENDLY
Flamingo

1

Paint your nails with two coats of the solid color. Wait for the polish to dry completely.

2

When the solid coat is dry, use the ball of the dotter to make a pink oval on the top right tip of your nail.

3

Leave some space between the neck and the edge of your nail.

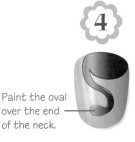

Starting on the left side of the oval, use the ball or point of the dotter to make a curved pink line shaped like an "S." This is the neck.

4

Paint the oval over the end of the neck.

Use the ball of the dotter to make a pink oval around the end of the neck — this is the flamingo's head. Let the polish dry.

5

For the eye, make a **big** white dot on the flamingo's head. Let the polish dry.

6

Draw a curved black beak with the point of the dotter. Then make a **small** black dot on the eye.

{ MIX AND MATCH
Try pairing your flamingo with a dotted design, like Confetti (page 18). }

FLAMINGO FACE OFF

It's easy to change the direction your flamingo faces.

1

Make the oval on the left side of your nail.

2

Reverse the neck by making a "C" curve instead of an "S."

3

Add the head, eye, and beak.

picture nails

{ Think of the designs in this section like puzzles. Each nail is a piece. Put the pieces together, and you see a complete picture. Genius!

S1 CITY Skyline

WHAT YOU NEED
- Polish for the sky
- Black polish
- Polish for the windows
- Dotter

1

pinky   *thumb*

Paint your nails with two coats of the sky color. Wait for the polish to dry completely.

2

When the solid coat is dry, use the point of the dotter to make a black line across each nail. This is the ground.

tip

To make a line, dab (don't drag) the dotter. It's OK if your lines aren't perfectly straight. You'll paint over them later.

3

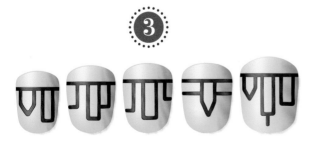

Use the point of the dotter to outline the buildings on each nail, also in black. Change the height and shape of the buildings from nail to nail.

4

Use the ball of the dotter to fill in the buildings and ground in black. Wait for the polish to dry.

5

Light up your city by making **small** dots on each building in the window color.

Shark
ATTACK!

1

Use the shark color to make three fins — gradually increasing in size — on your ring, middle, and index fingers. First, outline the fins with the point of the dotter, then fill them in with the ball.

2

Outline the head with the point of the dotter, then fill it in with the ball or brush.

Now, make a large triangular shape on your thumb. This is the shark's head. Wait for all the polish to dry.

3

Your waves don't need to match the picture exactly.

Make waves along the tip of each nail, using the point of the dotter to outline and the ball to fill in. Make sure the waves don't cover the fins.

4

On your thumb, use the point of the dotter to make a black crescent shape for the mouth.

5

Make two **big** black dots for eyes. Wait for all the black polish to dry.

6

Let the mouth dry before you add the teeth.

Use the point of the dotter to make tiny white triangles for teeth. If you have trouble, make **small** dots instead.

Lovebirds
ON A WIRE

① thumb / pinky

Paint your nails with two coats of the sky color. Wait for the polish to dry completely.

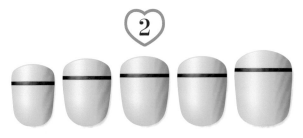

②

When the polish is dry, use the point of the dotter to make a black line across each nail, near the tip. This is the wire.

WHAT YOU NEED

- Polish for the sky
- Black polish
- Polish for the beak
- White polish
- Polish for the heart
- Dotter

USE A STICK-ON STENCIL

If you're working with regular polish, try using stick-on stencils to make the wire. Stick the first stripe on your nail evenly. Then line up the second stripe just a little below the first one.

Paint this space, overlapping the stencil edge a little.

Paint the area between the stencils with two light layers of black polish, then remove the stickers immediately. Voilà! A perfect line (see page 49 for more tips on using stencils).

ACCENT FINGER

This next part is a little tricky. You may need to practice it a couple of times. Start by choosing your accent finger. The lovebirds usually look best on your index or ring finger.

1

Leave some space between the ovals for heads and beaks.

Use the ball of the dotter to make two small black ovals that angle slightly toward each other at the bottom.

2

The tails start at the top of the ovals and angle to the sides.

For the heads, make a **big** black dot at the bottom of each oval. Then use the point of the dotter to make two short black lines for tails.

{ Try putting the birds on different fingers with hearts between them.

3

Use the point of the dotter to make two teeny tiny orange dashes for beaks. See below for tips.

4

Using the point of the dotter, make a tiny white dot on each bird's head. Eyes!

5

Now, for true love... Use the point of the dotter to make two **small** pink dots right next to each other. Then make two short lines to connect the dots. A heart!

{ **MAKING DELICATE LINES & DOTS**

Don't put a lot of polish on your dotter — just dab it into the drop on your palette.

Touch the dotter to your nail gently, slowly increasing the pressure until you make the line or dot you like.

TROPICAL Beach

①

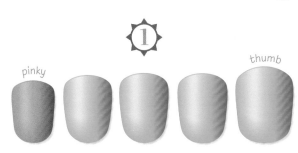

pinky

thumb

Paint your thumb, ring, middle, and index fingers with two coats of the water color. Then paint your pinky with two coats of the sand color. Wait for the polish to dry completely.

②

For a thicker tip, use the ball of the dotter.

When the polish is totally dry, use the point of the dotter to paint the tip of each blue nail with the sand color. Dab carefully, making a line along the edge of the nail. This is the beach.

tip

Painting French tips can be a little tricky. You may find it easier to use the stencils with regular polish (see page 56).

THUMB

 ①

The sun goes on the outside edge of your thumbnail.

Use the ball of the dotter to make a half-circle on the side of your thumb in the sun color.

②

Using the same color, make short lines around the sun with the point of the dotter. Wait for all the polish to dry.

③

In the middle of the sun, use the ball of the dotter to make a small half-circle in the sun accent color.

INDEX FINGER

①

Use the point of the dotter to make five black lines just below the middle of your nail. These are the palm tree leaves.

②

Make the trunk thicker near the sand.

Still using the point of the dotter, make a black line from the leaves to the beach. This is the tree trunk.

PINKY

①

Use the ball of the dotter to make two pink ovals for flip-flops. Wait for the polish to dry.

②

Now add straps. Use the point of the dotter to make two small, black lines on each flip-flop.

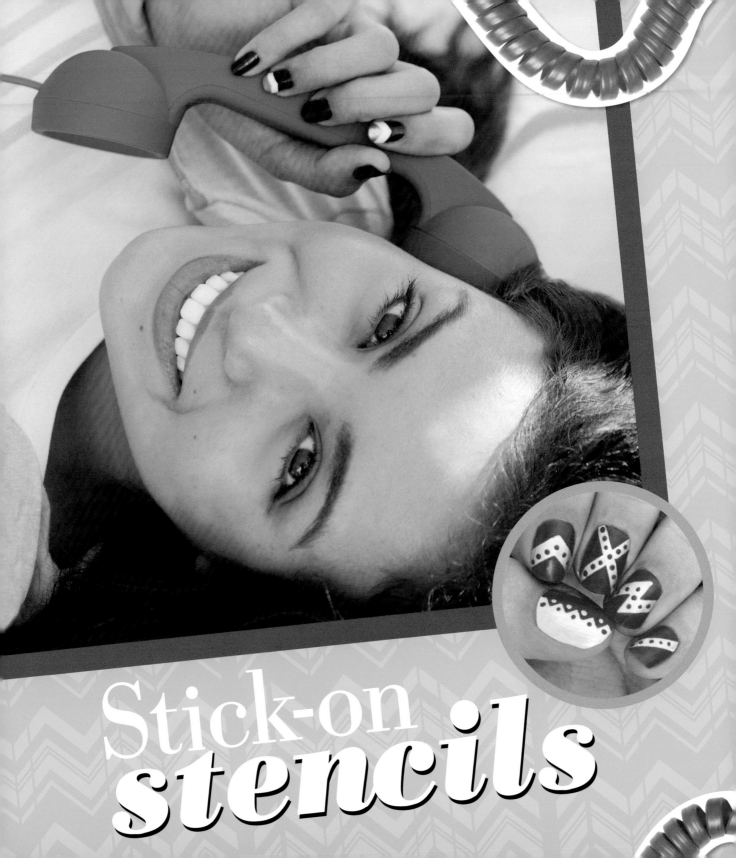

Stick-on
stencils

Stencil
BASICS

Stick-on stencils help you make crisp lines and shapes that would be difficult to draw free-hand. The stencils are simple to use, but you do need to follow these basic guidelines.

A NOTE ABOUT POLISH

The yellow stick-on stencils do not work with the practice polish that comes with this book. **You can only use the stencils with regular nail polish.** Be sure to get an adult's OK before you use regular nail polish.

1 Start each stencil design by painting your nails with a solid coat of polish (you may need two for some designs). Let the polish dry **completely** — at least 15 minutes.

2 When the polish is absolutely, totally, definitely dry, peel the stencils off the yellow sheet and stick them on each nail. Make sure to press the edges down firmly so no polish gets underneath.

3 Follow the directions to paint the nail design. **Don't use a lot of polish — a light coat works best.** Wait for the polish to dry.

4 Add another light coat of polish as directed, then remove the stencil **immediately**. This is very important — if left on too long, the sticker will pull up the polish.

You can only use a stencil once. Stick used stencils on a piece of scrap paper while you finish your manicure. Throw away the paper when you're done.

5 If your lines or shapes are uneven, let the polish dry, then use the point of the dotter to touch up the edges with the same color polish as the shape.

SLEEK Stripe

WHAT YOU NEED

- Polish for the stripe (avoid dark colors)
- Polish for the main color
- Polish for the dots (optional)
- Stripe stencil
- Dotter

1

This color will become your stripe later on.

Paint your nails with a coat of the **stripe** color. Wait for the polish to dry completely.

2

Press the edges of the stencil all the way down.

When the polish is totally dry, stick the stripe stencil on your nail in any position you like. If you're stenciling your other nails, sticker them now.

Try mixing horizontal and vertical stripes.

③

Paint your nail with the main color, covering the stencil. Let the polish dry. Add another coat...

{ You can alternate stripe color and direction from nail to nail. Using the same main color will bring the design together.

④

...then peel off the stencil **immediately**, revealing the stripe.

⑤

If you want, make **small** dots on the stripe in any color you like.

SUPER STRIPES

For a little flair, paint your nail above the stencil a different color from your nail below the stencil. Paint the second coat one nail at a time, removing the stencil before going on to your next nail.

Paint a little over the edges of the stencil.

DOTTED X

WHAT YOU NEED

- Polish for the X (avoid dark colors)
- Polish for the main color
- Polish for the dots (optional)
- Stripe stencils (2 per nail)
- Dotter

1

Paint your nails with a coat of the **X** color. Wait for the polish to dry completely.

Lightning BOLT

WHAT YOU NEED

- Polish for the lightning (avoid dark colors)
- Polish for the main color
- Lightning stencil

1

Paint your nails with a coat of the **lightning** color. Wait for the polish to dry completely.

2

Press the edges of the stencil all the way down.

When the polish is totally dry, stick the lightning stencil on your nail. If you're stenciling your other nails, sticker them now.

2

Press the edges of the stencils all the way down.

When the polish is totally dry, stick one stripe stencil on your nail diagonally. Add another stripe stencil to make an "X." If you're stenciling your other nails, sticker them now.

3

Remember, a light coat works best.

Paint your nail with the main color, covering the stencils. Wait for the polish to dry. Add another coat...

4

...then peel off the stencils **immediately**, first removing the top stencil (the second one you added), to reveal the X.

5

If you want, make **small** dots inside the X in any color you like.

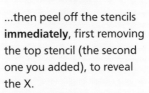

3

Remember, a light coat works best.

Paint your nail with the main color, covering the stencil. Let the polish dry. Add another coat...

4

...then peel off the sticker **immediately**, revealing the lightning.

Give your manicure pizazz by making horizontal and diagonal zigzags, too.

ZANY Zigzag

1

Paint your nails with two coats of the lighter color. Wait for the polish to dry completely.

2

Press the edges of the stencil all the way down.

When the polish is totally dry, stick a zigzag stencil on your nail in any position you like. If you're stenciling your other nails, sticker them now.

3

Remember, a light coat works best.

Paint your nail on the zigzag side with the darker color, covering the edge of the stencil. Let the polish dry. Add another coat...

{ For this look, paint a zigzag on your middle finger. Then paint the nails on each side in their matching zigzag colors. }

4

...then peel off the stencil **immediately**, revealing the zigzag.

5

Make **small** dots in the corners on both sides of the zigzags using the contrasting color.

FRENCH Tips

1

Paint your nails with two coats of the main color or clear base coat. Wait for the polish to dry completely.

2

You may need to scrunch the stencil to get the right curve.

When the polish is totally dry, stick the crescent stencil just below the tip of your nail, matching the natural curve of your nail. If you're stenciling your other nails, sticker them now.

3

Remember, a light coat works best.

Paint the nail above the stencil, covering the edge of the stencil, too. Let the polish dry. Add another coat...

4

...then peel off the sticker **immediately**, revealing the French tip.

STAR & Heart

This design looks best as an accent — or on only a couple of nails, as shown in the photo.

WHAT YOU NEED
- Polish for the main color
- Polish for the heart or star
- Heart or star stencil

1

This will be your background.

Paint your nail with two coats of the main color. Wait for the polish to dry completely.

2

Throw out this piece.

Peel up the heart or star stencil. Poke out the shape and throw it away.

tip The star stencils are right next to the hearts on the stencil sheet.

3

Press down the inside edges of the shape, too.

Stick the stencil on your nail however you like. Smooth it out and press down the edges.

4

Paint over the edges of the stencil shape.

Paint your nail in the middle of the stencil with a light layer of the heart or star color. Let the polish dry. Add another light coat...

5

Use the point of the dotter to touch up the shape with a little polish.

...then peel off the stencil **immediately**, revealing the heart or star. Lovely!

GRAPHIC Chevron

1

Paint your nails with a coat of the **chevron** color. Wait for the polish to dry completely.

2

Press the edges of the stencil all the way down.

When the polish is totally dry, stick a chevron stencil on your nail. If you're stenciling your other nails, sticker them now.

3

Remember, a light coat works best.

Paint your nail with the main color, covering the stencil. Let the polish dry. Add another coat...

4

...then peel off the stencil **immediately**, revealing the chevron.

SNAZZY CHEVRON

Try painting your nail above the stencil a different color than your nail below the stencil. Paint the second coat one nail at a time, removing the stencil before going on to your next nail.

Paint a little over the edges of the stencil.

{ Try alternating colors from nail to nail.

Credits

DESIGNER
Jenna Nybank

ART DIRECTOR
Maria Corrales

EDITOR
Anne Akers Johnson

INSTRUCTIONAL ILLUSTRATOR
Jim Kopp

DECORATIVE ILLUSTRATOR
Andi Butler

PHOTOGRAPHER
Rory Earnshaw

NAIL DESIGNERS
Eva Steele-Saccio, Onnesha Roychoudhuri,
Rebekah Lovato Piatte, Natasha Polak

PACKAGE DESIGNER
David Avidor

PRODUCTION COORDINATOR
Kelly Shaffer

PRODUCTION EDITOR
Madeleine Robins

PRODUCTION DESIGNERS
April Chorba, Quillon Tsang, Jill Turney

EDITORIAL ASSISTANT
Rebekah Lovato Piatte

MANICURIST
Lily Huang

Special thanks to DeWitt Durham, Barb Magnus,
and all the great polish testers at Klutz.

Photo Credits: Page 8: Painting nails © Maurizio Chiocchetti/iStockphoto; Page 16: Soap bubbles © Sergii Dibrova/iStockphoto; Page 19: Traditional lace © Zoran Kolundzija/iStockphoto; Page 24: Daisy © Malerapaso/iStockphoto, Strawberry © Ranplett/iStockphoto; Page 26: Streamer © Hans Slegers/iStockphoto; Page 32: Colorful Sweets © Spaxiax/ Shutterstock; Page 32: Candy Stars © Shebeko/Shutterstock; Page 33: Cherry © MistikaS/ iStockphoto; Page 34: Fly © Marc Fischer/iStockphoto; Page 35: Pink & Red Shoelace © Khouwes/iStockphoto; Page 38: Pink Flamingo © Suzannah Skelton/iStockphoto; Page 47: Thongs © Subjug/iStockphoto; Page 48: Phone Cord © DNY59/iStockphoto; Page 51: Soda pop © Doug Cannell/iStockphoto; Page 56: Lemon © Dimitris Stephanides/iStockphoto

Here are more Klutz books we think you'll like.